KISMAT

किस्मत

FORTUNE. FATE. DESTINY

AARAV CHOPRA

AARAV CHOPRA

For Ma,
thank you for *always protecting*
and never quitting on me. You are my hero.

I will never question why I chose to love words
more than numbers.

Words have given me the freedom to explain
myself in ways I can't count.

But.
I can write.

CONTENTS

K

I

S

M

A

T

Ek Kahani

एक कहानी

ONE STORY

KISMAT

I am now living with greater positivity in my life thanks to the helping hand of family, friends, and honest acquaintances. I can also thank the fruitful benefits of time as well.

Once I began to stop asking for something different about my life I learned to appreciate my being. I realized that every year, month, week, day, hour, and every second of this life I will always be the person my mother brought into this world.

I learned to appreciate my *small brown eyes, average nose, big ears, long fingers, long arms, long legs, and my dark complexion* to live.

To live this one story -
And to live it my way.

Welcome to the mosh pit of fate.

AARAV CHOPRA

I am a river to see,
But an ocean to remove.
You can play in my streams,
By night the waves will devour you.

I am a body awaiting sentence.
Let the moon show all my bones,
Let the stars pretend to be my home.

Everyday you speak to my demons.
My angels schedule your play dates.

Never stop motivating her.
Be relentless.
for you don't know how much she needs it.

The mirror has always always been a private moment for me.
A reflection so human I have to pinch my skin to believe.

For the glass half full after my spill.
Where there's a will there's a way –
Whatever remains will suffice to fill.

AARAV CHOPRA

You've fallen. You've risen.
You've lied. You were forgiven.
You bled. Yet you healed.
Even through all of this...
You can feel.

KISMAT

How does it feel to be home?
All dressed down - the freedom of being alone.
In the kitchen creating a dinner for one.
Open a bottle of wine just to feel a little buzzed.
Forget that you have an endless amount of work to do.
Just don't pickup the phone when they're calling you.
You're home.

The winds that make you shiver are a message from the sins you left on my skin.

Fade to black like you absorbed all the light.
Embrace the darkness that shakes others at night.
Not to scare but to relate.
With those who have yet to see their brightest day.
You are not as holy as the light that makes you feel warm.
You are only a being that can bring calm to those who feel as if
they don't belong.

*You are the warmth against their shiver, for you never judged a
scar you never shared.*

A lot can happen when you branch out and show that you care.
You may not be someones light, but you can be apart of their
darkness to help their good fight.
Each step...each step.
Will bring you both to light.
Fade to light.

Slowly you'll prove your worth.
It's possible in your lifetime.
You will gain who you deserve.
Understand the situation and be flexible with the plans.
No matter what give it your all, this is your only chance to live.
You may get many chances for other things but your heartbeat
only stops long enough to prove it's all said and done.

Once

You won't know. You won't care.
You could have been selfless.
Or a sinner with your eyes red.
Souls rest eternally not without their tests.
Keep on strong leave some memories, no regrets.

Don't dress to feed the stallions and dames. One may judge
you by brand but they'll never try you on for size.
Be you.

I do. You don't.
I can. You can't.
I am. You aren't.
I remind. You forget.
I miss. You regret.
I make it. You break it.
I say it. You disobey it.
I start it. You end it.

I still love what you do for others, for it's more than I do for
myself.
That's why you tipped my scales after so many years of denying
my health.
I'd stop my vices –
Just to keep on sharing these moments with you.

DIAMOND DOVES *featuring J. Saunders*

I told you I'm not the one to sit and love myself.
Fulfilling your fantasy life.
You loved more of me than I could ever trust you to love.
Have you always looked after me like a diamond dove?
Just to clip my wings.
You fed me the taste of your past to watch me sing.
I've known the tempest in you.
I gave you a chance to become clear sky blue.
Looking for others you opened the cage.
I escaped you, heartbreak, and rage.
I dive.
Free falling back to my elevation.
Yes dear, I'm far above you now.

-

A.Chopra

I trembled in fear unsure of the unknown.
what could live beyond the cage you entrapped me in.
I deserve love in my future only to jump
for the freedom to sing my own song.
To create my own blue sky.
I am not just flying but soaring above all I thought
was impossible. Loving myself was the impossible...
It was.
It was....
Not anymore.

-

J.Saunders

GODS CREATION

Running through the breeze.

Trust me I know it's cold outside but baby let's wait till we go inside.

There's no telling what we might do.

I'm just glad I'm running through the world next to you.

Blood rushing through our veins but the love is pumping through our brains.

We love each other and that's all that we have come to know.

Each day I wake up and smile – knowing that you're laying next to me and our love grows.

Life isn't always what it's made up to be but if you're next to me I'll be okay.

You're mine now and I hope it continues to remain this way.

Please my love let's run through the night and reach our final destination.

When we get home there's nothing more than love rushing through us for this is what God wanted from his own creations.

To love.

I am not the postage stamp that was cleared to let the message
get to you.
I am in the ink that remains in the letter that was
addressed to you.

KISMAT

She was hidden in the room.

Not behind her makeup or clothes.

But from the invisible scars left from the men in her past I suppose.

They'll look at you in the morning as you get to work and wonder
why a flower rests so peacefully in your hair.
Little do they know it was a present from me to grant you a
renewed feeling of fresh air.
It will wilt away that I know - but until it does let it show,
The freedom you had with me the night before.

KISMAT

Close your eyes and live.
Pass your lips to show you forgive.
Go ahead and undress the way you do, to give justice to your
hips.
Rid me of the tensions and do all the things that I missed.
It's been awhile since I've had you to myself and there's plenty for
you to say but you chose my name.
I'll take what you say as a response to the actions I'm
committing with no shame.
The embers in the fireplace have matched to our hearts.
Before we opened the door we weren't aware these covers would
be the only thing keeping us from drifting apart.
Remember that on every starry night I loved you from the start,
Till death do us part.

You got me physically and then you took away my bad mental-
ities.
You made me go back and make room for such a reality.
I thought I ran out of empty spaces but I rid my past for you to be
a part of me.
Your origins confirm my actions and for that I need an elixir –
your poison was stronger than most would believe.
My heart lost desperately and I decline all further
questions for me.
I let go of all my emptiness and finally had enough space for you
in me.

KISMAT

Broken bones crushed away for currency,
the new crushed cans. Tomb raiders galore anti humanity acts
scorching our Earth. Purging never felt so real.
Fast forwarding to a time I never want to bleed.
Sharks all around clenching their teeth.

I want to find you away from the herd.

There's many of us...

Humans.

Walking around throwing their self worth like coins in a well.

Caught under a bad spell. leaving it to luck to escape their hell. I mean the well.

I want your spells. potions. and emotions. Trade for all of me, here's to the one I've chosen.

I'm **agile** I'll love you from every spot in my heart.
I'm **tactile** my decisions are made to help you figure it out.
I'm **worthwhile** I'll stay by your side. we won't be apart.

My eyes weren't filled,
That was only the light bidding for its sake of my attention.
That glow you speak of -
I have seen it before.
But your attention begs for dedication and I may not want to
commit to that yet,
The sun -
Now the sun would be pleased with that decision.

Your beauty hasn't been defined,
So I will love you with the words I know.

You will still matter where you belong.

KISMAT

Come here babe let's see your tattoos.
Let's take a closer look at the pain when I wasn't there for you.

I love music so much.
I wish I could remix people —
But I don't know the sound of their soul.

I gave her a brush to paint.

She then drew under her eyes.

Said she needed more than her daily mascara that day.

Something more permanent.

Something more toxic.

Just to match her emotions.

To be open to other options.

She was tired of spending the time to put it on right.

For she knew it would come rolling down her eyes by the end of the night.

You asked for love when she was on her knees.

Imagine if that were the only image of love she could believe.

Now every night her tears stain her face black as she sleeps.

When you begin to realize who you were before it,
that's when you know you are addicted.

I'm the opposite of a eulogy - I declare that I'm alive.

I won't accept your labels you won't know how to handle me.

He felt weak only to hear.
Close quarters meant something different when she was around.
He could let his guard down.
For she was able to bare the burden of her crown.
He knew what she was capable of.
Like a chess piece he set his troops aside and earned her love.

Her kingdom didn't have to fall.
He didn't have to ruin his.

Greatness beckons the name of the beholder.
Beauty rests in their eyes.
Merry go round -
Sit me down.
Now I fail only by surprise.
I'm just not myself -
Balancing think tanks and bad funks.
Shaking the energy out one way.
Knowing the ending will be positive.
I'm no negative.
I've slept face down on plate as a child,
I knew what it meant to be tired then.
I knew defeat losing things in playgrounds and then paycheck
taxes.
It happens to all of us.
But to me, and I hope for you too –
When I get in a situation of loss,
I've found that I profit somehow after time sends me the proper
opportunity cost.

KISMAT

I'll be there for your success as if it were mine.
Remember that even at your lowest point –
Together we'll be fine.

THE DUNGEON

I've crawled back into the places I call home.
Weak and hungry my body is tense due to all the stress in my
bones.
My thoughts don't save me like they use to.
They keep me up at night and there's no one out there to talk to.
I feel lonely. Broken into pieces when I crawl into bed.
I understand the emotions but the truth is I can't begin to fathom
what goes on in my head.
The trust I've had in others tends to fade quicker than the smoke I
exhale. The second I begin to surface from the darkest side of my
soul I find new demons surrounding me and into their dungeons
I go.
I'm struggling to find my happiness. I'm struggling to find the
memories when I want to reminisce.
There's nothing left for me to seek when I'm locked away for so
long. There's nothing left for me to keep when I've been giving for
so long.
Should I give up on my soul to the darkness that has consumed
me? Should I break free of their control and try to find myself
again? The answers are not clear. I just want to be whole again but
the outsiders are my biggest fear.
Who am I outside these walls I call home?
Who am I to these strangers I don't know?
What do I do when I don't know what to say?
What will I do with myself come judgment day...

He worked on behalf of her.
Set his winnings aside to watch her gather hers.
He gave her the light she needed to bloom. No wonder why he's
her perfect groom.
She can be first he said,
Without her —
He saw no reason to get ahead.

Escaping sobriety we want to feel the world,
through our liver and lungs.
Just to encourage our hearts to think differently.

Cold.   Shaken.   Stirred.

        Drunk.   Vision.   Blurred.

                Body.   Weak.   Numb.

    Who have I become?

There will always be someone out to get you.

If you don't pick up on that life lesson, it'll be over soon.

Remember that chasing success isn't an act done alone or without competition.

Unless, you can create wealth, health, peace and

happiness you must work well with others to escape the oppression.

An artist doesn't have a broken reality.
The parallels they draw were for you to see.

I need you for you,
No creamer and no extra sweet.
Just like you everyday,
Presentable by your smile, oh so neat.
Believe me I can tell some change from a dime.
I've been trying to find something different than a corny pickup
line.
Tell your feelings I can't harm you and I've made my
decision. I've been silent from you this long, guess I've met my
limit.

KISMAT

You can't reach my love throwing a rope over the wall
around my heart.
Sooner or later your arms will get tired.
Just like the others –
Their rope wasn't enough.
No strings should be attached.
I can see over my wall.
If you're an honest lover,
I'll let you through.

Hit the brakes before the tab splits into your mind.

Something to secrete in your nerve endings.

Let it stay with you until you recall what sobriety doesn't mean for you.

The marble floors explain more to your success than the dosage does.

Do the white collars strike fear into your antibodies?

They do...don't they?

Sedated for success.

I've heard of this before.

The strong carry on until their mind loses balance.

Chemically they bring themselves back.

Hours spent, many hours spent that you'll never get back. Unless in cash.

Exchanged for money their damage has been done -

Go home.

We might be thinking about three sides of the story.

My side.

Your true side.

Then the one that puts you in for the glory.

I know your kind.

You tend to fabricate to your seniors to prove to them
you're golden.

I don't care for that side.

If that is how you fold your cards when you're dealt them.

The anger will resonate as you melt them.

For I'll save them from your flames with honest acts my
good man.

See you're no failure to me but this is your tragedy.

I conquered them by doing the only thing they look forward to
from their colleagues.

Honesty.

I have the slightest idea what true love is anymore.
I've heard from liars, cheaters, and others who said they opened
loves door.
They can work with merit but choose to love with secrets.

I do not agree with anything that isn't transparent.

I haven't been in a relationship for a long while. It's been more than a couple years since my first one, my only one so far in life. I've felt the same way about love since the sorrows of the break up steeped through me long enough. It took my brittle mind a long time to heal. Truth be told, I only begin to sink when I think of all the serious close quarters physical interaction involved with love as a concept.

My fear was known to her as well. For I didn't love lightly, and she knew. I knew what passion was and she knew too. It's difficult to replace the passion when it's your strongest memory of love.
-

The term, "single," irritates the living hell out of me sometimes. The idea to be carried by so many integral parts of life like your mind and body should not limit the help from others. I have been single for well over four years now and I have learned more about relationships removing myself from one. The dynamic changes very quickly as you fly by your 20's.

I have found that removing labels in certain social situations changes the dynamic of more than you would quietly assume.

There is love. There is love. Never will I say you can't attain that.

I have one heart,
I wish only the best for many others daily –
but seldomly my own.

KISMAT

Once you leave,
Leave out more than just love.
Just remember to keep some love there at the end.
As a reminder that once its all over, you can still have some
leftover to make amends.
You mustn't abandon your heart too.

You aren't the galaxy they spoke of.
You weren't even a star -
You were just another human acting the part.

The hunting begins at dawn.
Rise before you become one of the fallen.

You spring these words, my year round season.
You were enough.
Like the few raindrops from the trees to let me cleanse myself
of the stains.
Many parts of you I want to keep the same.
Elements of you I cannot squander, into you I wander.
Daily I praise, deep into your wanderlust.
I am saved.
Hoping with my care.
You can be too.

My marvel.

My hero.

Independent to the end.

There is no equal.

I have yet to see.

One as strong as you.

Identifying your days as good while the others label them bad.

Milk and honey ripen a soul.

Stress has yet to remove you from its control.

But you won't even budge.

Not even a little.

My marvel.

My hero.

Always telling me there's a step one.

When I tell you I am down to zero.

Simply surveying the indecencies wasn't enough for my eyes. I
won't speak to what I saw but I will scribble it down in a book
you'll never find too.
I've been to where the blue berries taste better than the aesthetics
of it's delivery.
Hand picked they say and their own recipe.
I can tell you I've tasted words as sweet as their sounds
off my tongue.
I heard lies in the air, I filtered them through.
Went on with my day, I took my trust and spoiled you.
I was the excuse after your cards ran out.
I'd help you problem solve if it was worth it.
Either way, I still failed you.
I should not risk my life anymore, after I've lost all my trust. The
being I am, the big things I've done.
Spoiled immediately I can no longer hang on.
Protecting your interests, I always did.
Saving your image as I've protected mine all along.
I only tried to save you.
For the thousand reasons I saved you from others, this one time
you found reason to regret.
You let me go on —
You'll easily forget.
Knowing me.

Remember the time the doors never opened even though you
mentioned you would be there on time.
Respectfully you had an urge greater than others but still seniority
took your place in line.
You awaited a key from a person who was trusted,
You worked hard to hold the keys that you always longed for but
what good is the key when the locks are now
rusted. Now tell me if you're working that hard...
Was it all worth it?
Sometimes you're early and present but for the world it's too late.

You said I was lying through my teeth.
Yet I was never as sharp as you.
I served your lies in bones.
You skinned the truth like meat.

Jumping from distance.
To the unknown of your past.
Collecting lost thoughts.
(a haiku)

I can tell that I believe you but trusting is not enough.
These stories you are telling me -

I was never there.
That's trust.

Forget them *darling*.
They are petty like red yield *signs*.
You know your *options*.
You can choose to let them *go*.

--

You aren't on a dedicated path and they aren't either. You can balance. You can redirect. You can stop them or you can go with them. So many ways to put it, but if they do not need to be with you: they can be passed on to society.

Let the silence patch your broken promises. Channel the positivity. See what happens when you go off path to leave them on another highway. For only awhile, or make your decision indefinite. Either way, you must be selfish and not put down.

It's everybody's common fear, keeping people in and out. As you mature you begin to realize constantly some are just there to be merry and others just want to see you turn around to go back. Don't turn around. Even if they speak best to your back. You don't have to face what you can paint in a lie.

Options. Go.

They want to be treated,
<u>Different</u>
They want to be touched,
<u>Different</u>
They want to be loved,
<u>Different</u>
They want to be remembered,
<u>Different</u>

But they treat you the same as the others who've left.

Now there's your difference

Take me as another who claims to spend his time with you and
acts like a dove flying delivering lust.
I've taken my time to await yours —
If you please, allow me to treat you well and never lose your trust.
I've flown for awhile, I am landing to seek what I've been pursuing.
Candles last longer than men and their scent you can't ruin.
I'm only here for awhile, or I can stay.
If you care to find love, I do too.
Let's both be honest to each other and stay.

The one who makes the save gets the last dollar from the man
who thought nothing was possible.

I'm the unforgiving enemy... the bitterness after your first sip fails
to please you.
Then I stay in your hands.
Remain in your mind.
For dropping me so easily wouldn't be done quietly.
I only asked if you wanted me to warm things up politely.

I was your type of love.

Although you, your love was pseudo.

I stumbled as I read your name, my name was on the
reservation list too but I invited only myself today.

I could see where you were with loving a man.

Enough of them are around town to say you should stay as
long as you can.

I wonder why he already rolled up his sleeves.

I can sense his lust focusing in.

I can see you itch your leg nervous, back heel with the opposite
heel. Forgetting the real pain for temporary relief.

One order ribs, medium well, serve the champagne cold.

Extra ice please.

That way. To her and him.

There you were, so was I.

I chose here too tonight, but with me you did not choose to dine.

The tabs on him.

Hope he still has his appetite.

Skin the rib eye, freeze the liquor.

My was love was true, your love defined bitter.

I've held onto our cold body...as your skin bared all the news.
The shivers you had a few times a night became something I
got use to.
I may have known how to put you to rest longer than you
would on your own,
But I gave up more of me than I should have right?
To be satisfied now by only sleeping alone.
I use to think the other side would never be as warm as it was
when you were the one who belonged.
Until I rid myself of the fever you brought along.

I haven't learned,
And I won't begin to.
I'm fragile. A bit broken.
Lost.
But, many have spoken about me.
It's been a lot to take in.
The fact that I'm all in –
To something I can't change.
But I am vulnerable.
That brings me to more pain.
I'm narrow minded but stand with a reach so far.
Sometimes I'm drifting yes, infinitely to the stars.
Remained grounded for as long as I can speak.
So many languages this story paints a fortune unforgiving to the
weak.
Resilience is what I've found.
Shattered but being put together.
I'm slowly finding my sound.
To peace.

Cutting up every piece of paper, write me again -
I'll recycle like paper.
I'll be the voice that returns after the pain has stopped
haunting you.
I'll be the piece of paper your will is written on.
I'll be the truth.
Yes, just me.
I can be -
The perfect ghost for you.

Goblets held in your name, aged, of course.
This wasn't new gold.
You never grew to live forever.
Your days in power went to sink away to bones, cement couldn't
write you a better goodbye.
These are written to engrave, the separation of your name.
From the best of me, to the lost soul in you —
You left me here.
I keep writing about you.

She wasn't the battlefield.
She was the fortress.
She was never in need.
She saw her final portraits.
For she cast her love to protect and guide you to all that you seek.
Hold her peace with you as an aura they cannot see.
Embrace her before you leave without your armor.
Continue to ward off those who seek to harm her.
Be her soldier.
For in her fortress out of every piece.
You are the most important boulder.

She is stardust,
Rising ether from the wells of youth and forgiveness.
Respectively she raises you too.
Don't worry -
The paths connect and appear if you do.
She sings the tune that makes the lemonade sweeter for the many harvests leftover in your mind.
She is no talisman, or a tell tale sign,
Just a human with a path you should align.

Hear.
The children in the playground screeching but still better
than nails on a chalkboard.
That's how I feel when I see them peaceful and their
parents are going back to the drawing board.
Arguments.
Mac and cheese for the kids while discussing the liver disease.
Careless drinking their brews.
In front of them.

Fear.
How will you make it all better when they've recorded that?
At a certain age.
Cost becomes more than the dollar.
You lose an opportunity to parent by losing yourself.
That's something your child can inherit.

Remember when you said hold on,
To only slip away from my grasp.
You sailed away.
Who was there to steer, when I held down the mast?
Gone with the wind.

Your cookie cutter dreams won't get filled by the men with their hands in cookie jars.

The law of attraction never prepares you for lawless deceit. The more you give the further you may sink beneath.

They are not to be loved like you should love a being like yourself.
You are forever changing to a story directed by yourself.
Create your life as one with a legacy.
You do not need to leave this world to look back at a legacy. Just
be there long enough to know you changed to make yours better
and better.

When you hold hands to feel together for the first time
is when you may seal the bond for an everlasting lifetime.
Now you won't know forever until you wear the band and never
want to remove it from your hand.
Forever theirs.

KISMAT

My hollow breaths brought warmth to your eyes.
So much so that you couldn't see beyond the cold in you.
I became the foundation to a cold blooded love.
All I had to do was bring the warmth.
All you had to do was be you.

I want to be numb next to you but want you to feel my emotions.
Not for pain but for sheer pleasure.
A little bit different this time,
I want you to feel my heartbeat ripped away from my veins. I
want you to know more about me than simply my name. I want
you to be there as I dance and sing about the terrible things as I
protect myself from the inglorious sins.
Do you feel my sorrow and happiness?
Measure me out explain the recipe –
For you've found my balance.
I'm no longer a soul left with reasonable doubt.
I've finally found someone that figured me out.

KISMAT

It's funny how easily I think of what was when the world says set the clock back one hour. I laugh in my own misery wondering who figured that out. Why not figure out the chemistry of humans. Impossible task albeit, for each day a new variable is born. I'm not asking for the variables to identify with me. I'm asking for one human to be the matching pair for me.

Something I've thought about for a long while now is the, "What if?" factor. Screw it right? It doesn't matter. Let it go. Move on. Fight the good fight. Be yourself and they too will follow. But how soon? How long from now? Today? Tomorrow? How long will I continue to feel for only myself in ways that it can jeopardize my mental health. What if my mind still hasn't learned the mating call or the words to procreate interest. Generating lost signals clouded in the smoke I continue to exhale to peak my form of serenity.

Whose there for me? Who can figure me out ... Who will truly set aside a part of their life to say this is the person ... this is the being ... that I was meant to save and love.

Until then...aren't we all just... soul searching?

There was no resolution, there was no change.
I've rearranged a couple things but nothing took me out of success' lane.
There's a path that leads to the riches above.
At times it will hook you, prepare for each dose like a drug.
For there are no wrong steps in this life you seek.
Just keep going forward and feel no reason to feel weak.
The path can claim all of you.
Just forget the darkness --
Follow the light in you.

KISMAT

The reverb kept calling everything sounded the same you see.
your sound was the only thing I needed but it was just. "I'll call
you later I promise you'll hear from me."
You never gave yourself the chance to believe in these helpful
hands you see.
I could work wonders -
But you never rang back to me.

Sometimes I creep up on an energy.
A rush through me that urges to take these long fingers of mine
and grab my neck.
Feel the suffocation to remind myself that the mystical pavement
laid framework for something God did not write all at once.
When one was created different than the soil they were
origin from.
That was changed to rewrite everything forever.
I only reach to the unknown which I know so little of.
Dark skies match my morning coffee and I bring the storm in me
for lighting in a bottle flashes through me enough.
Floating away from land, hostile in my own state.

Life is a constant chess game.
Either make the final move or utter the words for mercy.
Chasing victory dripping throat thirsty.
Drugs leave me woozy, wash the pain away find that leftover
whiskey.
What's the plan...where's the plug at?
Am I here to minus the seconds leftover in my clock.
Sober isn't how I enjoyed my thoughts.
I never called it my latest addiction for my ability to switch up
was always recently bought.
Stock up the substantial needs and forget the needful things.
Somewhere out there the red and blue lights are chasing me
behind the wheel.
I wouldn't be here if I didn't escape them -
This is how it feels.
Cigarettes and expensive thrills.
Alcohol and towering bills.
Exotic vibes in bed waking up to feel dead inside again.
Walk over to the mirror splashing water on my face.
Another reckless night I survived the race, leftover taste of last
night's pace.
Call that -
Check mate.

Separate your hate from patience and understand quality.

KISMAT

If I'm so sweet
Why did you let me ripen for this long?
Soon I'll be bitter.

I saw through the nerve to love her forever more.

KISMAT

Words describe journeys.
But without a compass -
How will you ever drop the anchor and find me?

Protect a story in your mind,
So only you know it's reality.

Is it cool to just open up and say that I'm hella heart eyes for you?
Or do I ponder and continue until you have a clue.

I want you to read to me,
With your tone and delivery.
Layered in your nerves are the chords,
String with your story or song.
Read to me in psalms,
Read to me feeling no stress in your palms.
As you traverse me through the pages you tell the time of
those in stories that never stop.
Counterweighting all that is wrong with my clock.
Visualizing a life in the world you and I are trapped in,
The secret life in your story delivered near my heart
within.

KISMAT

Can I be the thin framed man chasing your love more than the
weight of the loss at the end.
Higher thoughts elevated belonging.
Forgetful of rifts and downfalls.
Only remembering your loving call.

Sitting alone.

Unaware of the rest...

Rest of these issues.

Trauma sinking into my mind.

They found me on the ground. Regretting nothing I am trying to
pick up these pieces somehow –

Waking up and not even remembering a sound.

Couldn't even care where I was other than I wanted out.

ER early morning.

Unconscious I was found.

Losing possessions or memories seemed easier when it was just
sitting in lost and found after a bad day in the playground.

But I never lost me.

This only added another story.

A cold case I can't replace.

Scars that were left without a trace.

Healing is what we are trained to do.

The human race.

Dried out like mason jars awaiting a fresh night of
happiness. Infused with liquid or with empty space to fill in the
herb. We are creatures of habit and tolerances.
Where are the lines that connect all of this?
Whose to say my imbalance is like yours.
I need to settle my scores.
On the table I sink them -
Off them I reroute them.
8 ball corner pocket. calling it on the corner while he
counts the cash.
Supplying them daily. still showing up to mass.
Call the hitman or sharpen your blades.
Slow roast this conversation until we get their names.
Power
Blood stains don't save families after all.
Those who deal. don't test your blood before you fall.

It was all fun and games until you made me think.
About feeling guilty through your words yet when it was all said
and done you were at fault in my ink.

Never upset a writer.

We create receipts of your deceit.
A stronger mind that you once considered weak.

Immortalize you?
Sure...
My thoughts are always free.

I see you reflecting on me.
Thank you for your faith in me.

A little misdirection goes a long way...

Getting really far out of your comfort zone makes you learn more about yourself than the doubt you escaped.

Sooner or later you'll finish what you started and ask yourself who signs you up for the next race.

You could sense my paranoia -
At least you knew that I was high with you.

Maneuvering through your skin.

Braille.

Birth marks like you said.

Feels good to know where they lay.

Your eyes are closed too.

Intimacy draws us near.

Grasping for something near and dear.

Ending up in covers.

Smothered.

Waking up next to each other.

Bed and breakfast together.

No room service just an island in a kitchen with some egg shells in hand.

Let them cook.

Sunny side up.

Understand before you reject.
Fix it before you toss it.
Try to say yes before you say no.

Either way...

Don't think too much.
Make the best decision overall or you can live to remember the
roots of your wrongs.
It's not really slim pickings.

You plant the seeds.
Some will grow -
Some will die as you go along.

They tell you to savor each drop but the glass always takes some
for itself.

Do you have to be remembered enough to remain a memory?

KISMAT

You can't cheat a bullet out of regret.
Load the chamber pass it on, Russian roulette.
We know where you go when you hide all alone,
Thinking how the trigger doesn't feel like the skin on your bones.

They set fire to the cigarettes you hid away.
They were only protecting themselves so they don't
become your ash tray.

He didn't come home last night... Was it because of me?
Or did he get in a fight?
But with who, if not me?
Reclusive I sit.
Wondering if the day will get better.
Rolling rocks and throwing them.
A metaphor for cheap drunks.
Park by the river.
Sit and watch as the tiny rocks and puddles show you
failure and the quickest end to minor success.
Plunking each rock to a new place.
Some skipping far away from where they were, others
falling too close to shore.
Are they too heavy to carry the weight of my intentions?
Throwing them further away than where I stand.
Many still never make it to the water.
They're stuck on land.
Teary eyed begging where's my man?
Did I promise to him everything I said I'd do knowing I can't.

Love is not perfect.
Who says love making can't be?

Don't
be
your
savior
if
that
means taking it all for you.
A
loaf
of
bread
split
three
ways
could
feed
more
mouths
than two.

This life was not my right until I learned how to fight for it.
She walked with me hand in hand only for so long until I began
to run.

Hate the alarm.
Love the grind.

A man without movement,
Is a man -
Left in his thoughts.

KISMAT

I haven't failed.

I've only accepted a task I will accomplish.

With or without fail? No.

I don't like either or situations.

I just want the best outcome.

Every time.

Win or lose? No.

This

Is

My

Will

To

Win

Deadlines don't mean paydays.

A season of winning doesn't guarantee you an ending you didn't deserve.

Lose stamina,
Never lose strength.

I just wanted to get high without rolling papers and herbs.
Just wanted to feel numb after the euphoria of love we observed.

I knew from afar.
She wore the silhouette of a bride.

Go outside.
Chase the vibes.
Find the truth to their lies.
There's freedom out there.
Go see it with your own eyes.

"Be as you wish to seem."

-

Socrates

Believe in existence.
Then find its meaning in you.

-

Aarav

KISMAT

The marks he left with invisible ink.
She scrubbed everyday wiping her makeup off at the sink.
She had it all to give yet he split her up.
Order up another drink - she needs to feel more whole than an
empty cup.

Couple empty bottles later she found her way.
Crying in my arms but mumbling his name.

Every touch revealed another clue -
She was mine to love but she overdosed on you.

I became the remedy for the murder he wrote.
For the heart left with no feeling.
I filled it with love & hope.

AARAV CHOPRA

THE CORE

There's significant beauty in her words that describe her past
before she speaks of it to me.
Last night was the first call and contact was made yes we agree.
Nothing physical.
All mental.
Engraving wisdom, exchanging turmoil
this is how it all went.
Care and happiness passed on as the goodnight gift.
Good morning leads to another day.
Snooze the alarm forget what they say.
Floating into the struggle once more we compose
ourselves to the core.
This was a test everyday, now it doesn't phase us anymore.

128

It's obvious at times,
Your eyes can't focus onto sunsets.
They fear the sunrise.
You want to be fast,
Fast asleep.
You don't know what silence is.
Or the freedoms you use to keep.
The mountain didn't have a map as it did once before,
You have to apply now to open some doors.
Deprived and never relieved.
Sleep is a priceless sense of therapy.
Now who can blink?
I know you can't.
Keep going, keep fighting, this will end soon and your
time will be coming.
The pillow was cool with you leaving and not coming back.
As always, sleep well, the work you did will pay you back.

I keep thinking about you, although, I really shouldn't.
You were caravanning through my body and you took your time
before your exit.
My love shouldn't be your tourist destination.
This reckoning doesn't have to be our death sentence.
Just don't love me again or visit my heart.
I no longer wish to be friends with repentance.

Of course we like new money.
Our cards change.
Our hands don't.

SCARECROW

I've found the shift.
Gearing like the mixer making dough for the night or the car
speeding to catch the light.
I missed my flight.
Empty coffee mugs stimulated hand grenades.
Had many in my life. threw many at the wall when things went
this way.
Nothing blew up, no.
Just left pieces everywhere.
Proving my arrogance and aggressive nature.
Where did I go?
Where did I leave pieces of myself for later?
I never tended to it all...
You did.
Now where'd you go?

Did you cross off a goal before you paid toll today?
Or have the smoke you said you'd have after you
crossed over that way.
Early morning stressing out the scent of disaster stricken
lands into your own car.
Your cologne didn't save you but everyone was high off
something in that bar.
11 am.
Late to work.
They ruined your direct deposit. you asked for her to put it on
your tab last night. You walked in on percs.
Texts reading. "Hurry up. you're missing out. Larry was called a
jerk."
"Jamie made out with Sally right in front of the clerk."
None of this inspired your smallest smirk.

Have you struck another before?

Be truthful, have you forced your hand on something that couldn't fight back?

Serious thoughts.

Conversations over cigarettes with war veterans.

They told me their eyes saw their reasons, triggers for each man.

Removing their boots to serve another's heritage,

Knowing damn well back home, their church shoes shined as they heard more passages.

They load their chambers to keep you safe in yours,

Clear on arrival, next they breach the door...

One, two...*gunfire*

Rest was up to their eyes.

Aftermath

Now I'm home safe they said, freedom was served, justice was found.

PTSD kicks their ass and there are some new ghosts in town.

Pop double if the pain increases...call this number to talk to this hourly staff -

The war took them, they fought their way back.

The temptation to forget something's are too high, maybe enough to regret,

This leaves me haunted in my head.

Salute to you soldiers, next rounds on me instead.

I woke up without scratches,
The freedom I have is different than the masses.
Some fear who we chose,
I fear what other nonsense will continue to be exposed.
When rebellion strikes be mindful of those who leave no stone
unturned.
They will take back from those who want to watch us burn.

We voted.
They counted.
Our future lost.

KISMAT

I've been running on my knees.
The blood trailed to help you see the past I keep.
I ask simply that you bandage the wound.
I'm bleeding out and you won't see me soon.
I live with a heart so empty.
I need a remedy.
I ask that you forgive me -
Can we live with new beliefs.

She sits between my arms asking what more can I do.
I held onto her like wherever you go, I'm going too.
Ride or die.

KISMAT

I want you to be over so we can listen to smooth tracks from the
North as they talk about their tings.
Sitting in the Bay Area awaiting another banner so for another year
we can sing.
Champions.
Faithful.
Believers.
Adjust the tempo scream yadada yee!
If I'm from the Bay Area and she's from another sea...
I don't mind either way.
I still want her next to me.

I've past time loving my thoughts and acting alone.
Cooking for the taste buds I know I can satisfy.
Feeling for the scars knowing that they belong there.
Understanding my limitations, not reaching beyond my grasp.
Forward into motion with a cautious mindset accepting my fears
not going back.
Unless to step away from danger.
For I don't accept the fall.
I've been ready for it.
I'm prepped to fall again.
Not willingly.
Who does?
I break dawn with silence everyday.
Step by step these parks are not cheerful when the children are
away.
Brings a different level of solace when you're alone with your
thoughts to manage.
Wind chilling through the leaves, trickling through my neck hairs
begging me to bundle up.
But for once, I need to feel this freeze.
For it's better than a fall.
I'm frigid and still,
Acting purely on will.

Freezing out my heart,
Waiting for you to thaw it out.

KISMAT

Show me there's a story to the things I take care of on
my own without help. Show me something different.
A reason to listen.
To someone else,
Rather than myself.
They say I am debonair, benevolent, never loquacious
unless to heal.
Chanting more words to say, "I can do this."
Knowing I have and will.
Teach me ways to care for you.
Embrace a body I never scripted all the way through.
Trace your scars without knowing their belonging but
accepting their fate.
Creating a meal you can smell to sit down with me until the
dishes are empty, washed, and put away.
I want to love your empty spaces and wash away
what was wrong.
Safely place in you my emotions, no longer trapped in
my mind alone.
Lay with me, this way of living makes me feel at home.

The closer you get,
the quicker they question -
Who are you to me?

In words said by those I call friends. I find new enemies.
In spaces where they think my eyes can't go.

The promise words are different for everyone.
We just use. "I love you."
As an excuse to get away with saying it too many times until we
truly mean it.
Over and over and over.

Ask yourself if you're proud until the lights go off.

You fold me into corners like leftover takeout.
Containing as much as you can until you want to
finish consuming.
You'll never order me this way again right?
If you didn't keep coming back every night.

SHADOW

I live like my hell is a poetic nightmare you would be
lucky to wake up from.
The dregs hang around my breathe sniffing the emotions
drowned out in the horrors.
Escaping like fleeting energy from a dying soul you'd gasp for air
thinking about striking a chance of luck.
Think I'd make it this far if I was just a good fuck?
No.
Reside in my pain like I do with my sorrows.
Keep them together and there's nothing left from me to borrow.
Hollow out the nature of my face in your eyes.
The story I've lived and seemingly tell you has been falsified
by the misfortune upon me.
My signs do not end my story.
You foreshadow my skeletons as if I collect them as pathways in
my journey.
I may live like I seek God in at least one person a day.
But the subsidiary consequences of tragedy linger on
my heavenly plead.
I get torn between my imagery and shatter into pieces with a
room full of clothes and no cot.
It is all exterior.
Hollow out my eyes.
I feel no drop of shame.
I only sleep between a rock and a hard place.
I never wish to see more than where I've landed.
See me for what's outside and feel for what's inside.
Drown in my eternity and takeaway my evil.
To cleanse my luck I am nearby you.

So preview the ending as I tell it to you visionaries speak of my
reckless abandon to a cheery soul of peace.

Pickup that dusty book on my shelf read ninety-three times over
remembering the positions I'd wrap myself in looking for help.
"The Secret."

My smile is wrapped behind the blessing that is you.

I am not hopeless. I am settled with my body but my
mind proves to be its own nomadic being.

Each scratch to my surface has brought upon a teary legacy.

I have wept.

Hugging only my arms.

Feeling like the days have only gotten longer and the truth has
surfaced.

I may wrap myself in the facade of what the good man is and
swallow only the taste of air while they cherish their ninety
three-year.

I leave fragments.

I only share them now to bodies I've parted secrets to.

Age my secrets.

I return to you, for you've aged them the most.

Blank like a sheet of paper I am no muse.

I can manifest a peace only found cured by your eyes near me.

-

Your Fragile Shadow

KISMAT

Graves will back the words of lost lives.
As honest prayers try to steal life back from the graves.
Once their gone we must remember them as our angels and
remain brave.

> Don't save them -
> They're saved in you.

Warm up my love. I can start melting hearts.
But why melt them when you can just make them sweat?
I've been melted before.
So don't tell me you love me then ask me why I play hard
 to get. I am waiting for your true signs of love -
The ones that I haven't loved yet.

KISMAT

One's bloodthirsty lifestyle is another's sacrifice.
History of art and war.

One thirsts for power -
The other ticks till their clocks final hour.

Bring duality to someone you'll be their perfect pair.
Bring loyalty to someone you'll always be there.
Bring royalty to someone -
Carry their name as one you would also wear.

KISMAT

You against the world.
Down in the dumps with the weight of life on your back.
Stress so heavy it threatens to break you.
Will you allow it to make you crumble -
Or get back up no matter how often you stumble?
Step by step you will push on to the end.
Failure isn't an option my dear friend.
I'm here to tell you to embrace this adversity let it fuel your fires.
Let them burn freely and light your rage.
Frustration and anger build.
Like an eye glass, focus your internal light.
Harness the power for it provides immense drive.
Day by day you'll crawl further out of the shadows.
And when you meet adversity again -
Silence your sorrows.
Take a deep breathe and understand you earned
each second you never borrowed.

When will we realize tomorrow is just procrastination
spelled another way?

Never look to anyone for ruining a life you are still in
control of.

Like tombstones in the rain,
We weren't meant to be blanketed.
Only when we're born.
Age knows there's a final sentence.
One way or another an old page is torn.
Then God sends another angel up so another can be born.

How long do we play make believe -
Let's start telling ourselves there are others out there to meet.

AARAV CHOPRA

The orchids grew in her name,
The purple color never withered away.
Her hands showed the proofs of growth,
You see she knew the test and labor of time,
To her orchids -
She was hope.

Spin the bottle to kiss the girl,
Drink the bottle to forget her.
Easy come, easy go -
The empty bottle hasn't seen your soul.
Love responsibly

She hid herself behind my eyelids.
Said, "Don't forget me. I know what you did."
I worried forever that I couldn't keep her away.
My glasses fit perfectly but she wore my eyes today.
Just to prove she can stay.

KISMAT

He then turned to see that she was running away.
A bit of space turned into an eternity - kingdom hearts.
I felt the pain of a heart stabbed clean with the first blow -
kingdom come from the start.
She was the assassin you feared as the days went by.
You knew her name but her theft was done under an alibi.

AARAV CHOPRA

You can't crown every king -
You shouldn't fill every throne.
You can't praise every queen,
They've been known to act alone.

There will always be blood before every war,
The peace is breaking like every shooting star.
We have stopped identifying ourselves as who we are,
Confounded by our own secrecy drunken thoughts at the bar.
Cigarettes stomped in the name of wasted time,
Cautiously fearing them as they sniff their white collar lines.

I'm no rebel.
I'm no hero.
I am not a saint.
Maybe the war starts here -
So is that really blood or is that paint?
Look beyond power and remove any freedom not in you,
If it needs power, seek your own.

I've been running around.
You can't tell me I'm no help.
I've spent enough time.
I've been listening to you like the news.
Maybe this isn't for me and dear it doesn't always
have to be about you.
I've felt despair before now I can see clear.
Forget any level of misunderstanding -
I was there, even when you chose to not hear.
Calling you out wasn't for you to see.
I've spent enough leaving you trails of disbelief.
I'm spent.

I've been away from those drugs - they hurt me enough.
The touching the feeling of love - hurt me so rough.
I'm not saying I'm sober enough - to love you this much.
I'm just saying there is a divide between us - and I blame my
bad luck.
So why am I hurting this much - drinking this much.
Guess I'm not thinking enough - of what we've become.
I've been using all the wrong things - to tell you I'm done.
I'm now saying I'm sober enough - to be clean and move on.
On.
On.
To be clean and move on.

KISMAT

I'm for the people who don't have a voice.
Soapbox status -
My choice.
Up to the plate,
Batter, batter -
Battery charges to those who throw their hands with hate.
Here's to the enemy I cannot protect, too many negatives
 in my thought banks you see.
Collecting every hate crime memory like one day that could be
me.
Either or was never the case,
When a life was lost and could not be replaced. To the scars one
didn't deserve and now they sit and trace.
A life they didn't lose but now can't face.

I learned that the scars sit above so they don't tell my bones. Is my body hiding the story to the harnesses of my soul so I'm not alone in pain.
My bones are in tact -
But with my mind I can't say the same.

KISMAT

You were the safest choice.
The final destination for the storm and I that night was
under one roof.
Yours.
You knew where I would run to -
I would rather be soaking with you.

I want her to be loved by my friends and family,
But put to bed by me.

Having to deal with the negatives in life alone at times hurt me the most during my growing pains. When it comes to me. I cannot explain my pain. So I never ask for help. I can tell you a few things about it but honestly I have sent so many people away in my life. I harmed them by reducing their passions and willingness to help me. I did that. All on my own.

Dealing with it all like an adolescent at times. asking myself many times :
Why me. why now. and why me again?

I never knew the value of togetherness until I ran away...

She said I never see you you're like a ghost in a shell,
I thought my life would never be like another movie you could
find dusted on a shelf.
She's right as she always is, I've risen against my enemies and have
forgotten my angels under a spell.
Procrastinating love to the one who gave birth to me,
I swear this is only for my mom to know that she is valued and I
just let all my pride swallow my envy.
The jealousy of the Mission Hills families,
I denied the satisfaction that was her arms and just went off at 18.
Told myself that I can make it and she would just have to wait to
hear from me.
No doubt that leaving her then ruined the family.
I could tell that I believe you but trust is not enough,
I could tell you I wrote those lines but that was just inspired by
my mothers tough luck.
I just want to get even before I get ahead next thing you know I
am lonely once again.
Emptiness next to me I rose up against all the wrongs,
For I caused them all along -
I did that in my head.
That's why I am choosing to stay and never leave your arms again.
Ma.

Incinerated parchment.
My wages were cashed and I'm still awaiting the spring
of your voice.
Book me in the sorrows of my weightlessness.
My paychecks don't match the sacrifices.
Of a distance so far —
I can't see you in front of my eyes.

KISMAT

Move me like water.
At your pace.
Tributaries left in your name.
Multiply you into more and rivers spoke of you.
I may have held you in my hands more than once.
Or maybe I have tasted you wet.
This stream of consciousness we share can't be reset.
Drip with me.
Flow with me.
Let's sink and swim peacefully.

You should sharpen another knife faster.
Yours was used many times today.
I've made dull the edges of your blade,
Through resilience -
I was made.

Fall on your sword to profess your love.

Slow me down near the creek,

Just a little further.

Be careful, the twist is your test now.

Super-sport tires low tread not fixed but damn we knew why.

Our "fixes" cost more than those needed fixes you know. Habits
that never went away,

People and family left us astray.

Hands on fourth gear now. Too fast to slow us down.

Professing my love to you seemed suicidal somehow.

A lot can happen in a little bit of time you know.

Drop down to second let it scare the streets,

Our point is here now. Your lipstick matched the calipers that
night,

The night we drifted safely into our next right.

A man and his car, a woman who knew power. Timeless moment,
indeed our finest hour.

We then gave up our fixes,

To ride on with the power of trust as our true addiction.

KISMAT

Fingers woven, my fingerprints gave me access then.
Whenever we desired
Apart from each other we never gave it up alone.
The ceiling stopped the feeling of you in my home, choked up in
the same blankets without you to hold.
But it was us and our energy then, and now we have split.
No ceilings now, I used them to bury that truth behind me.

She balanced what I couldn't weigh.
I felt things were a little too left and you know it...
She made it all right.
She took her time with me.
I like it when she's blunt.
She won't blind me with false hope.
That doesn't make the warrior.
The reminder of pride and a reason to fight does.
I'm not alone without ammunition.
I'm balanced by her dedication.

KISMAT

I have lived and lived and lived; haven't you?
How glorious you are, you've aged well, haven't you?
Cannot place you in a bottle, oh heavens no.
I can only pretend to know if I will know more about you.
The darkness that consumes you.
It attracts me...it really does believe me −
If there is any light left over in you.
Your darkness will welcome me too.

Don't stand for every achievement until you've surpassed
your own expectations.
If you had none to begin with you shouldn't get lost
with empty superstitions.
One good thing may lead to another –
But one shouldn't stop when they've satisfied their
hunger. Seek more - Don't just get by with what they set as the
cover. Seek the path that takes care of you above and beyond
with your others.

– – – –

Make sure the people around you that lift your soul are rewarded
along the way. Simple thank you's go a mile. Thoughtful reminders
with gifts and treats done in other ways last a lifetime.

You remember the silence more than my name.

It's 4:00pm and I'm thinking of you. Not a drop in conversation I've been writing my own fantasies in my head. It's a shame really. Mother always said never believe in make believe. Yet, I do. I will along the paths of empty empty Fremont February's. Every year I come along a journey in my head. February 12th means something new to me every year.

He fell apart. He came back together. He got older. He forgot something good to gain a few more bad to learn the hard way. But here I am forgetting it all.

Forgetting that all I did as wrong was replaced at 4:00pm and I'm thinking of you.

KISMAT

You act the same,
Just to exhale my name.
I promise to not be the smoke,
And disappear.
But I can light your fires,
Leave a scent you'd admire.
I'd be damned if I was a liar.

I have visions of perfection.
I thank my eyes for witnessing the flaws.

PHOENIX

Let a couple things go.
The past couple of days let me know.
A cold shoulder never turned away someone who was already
shaking at their knees.
The fear of your past cannot foresee.
The future you wrap with your past you shouldn't believe.
It's a new day forget the bones you already laid.
Don't keep digging away at misery and ask to be saved.
Let experience be your teacher and your past be a substitute. Live
for now. your future has had enough with each excuse.

When she removes her armor what do you see?

You don't want to feel her emptiness do you...

Would you accept her scars before she points them out.

Will you hear her voice when she passes on the story left on her bones to you.

Don't collect her like the others.

She has shed her armor to gain access to limitless protection.

A bond.

Her stories may burn you but accepting her now and not meaning it will scar you.

Will you take care of what she offers?

Will you promise to resonate with her freely?

She has only one request don't retreat.

Create a bond in her bones, welcome her home.

Forge your armor with her, strengthen her journey.

Remember this tale began with acceptance, if you've offered her that please don't lose track of that memory.

Sacred places were broken for me. Reflections in the mirrors we both looked to for closure. Ready for the day ahead? Yeah. I am. Reminded more of what was and what tomorrow will look like knowing today I recalled your sight again. It's painful. I can't hold onto that side of you anymore. I can no longer go there and act brand new. Others do. I can't. A lot of me me me in my thoughts you see. My actions brought you near me and these sacred places were now seen by you. Pitiful that they mean nothing to me now. Long walks to remember smaller stories with bigger details slower pace. Winds that chased us and our hands kept us together in place. Glance back this way just once the soundtracks rewinded back to help us relax. Scary how this is all a memory of what I asked you to forget. I remember too much old love. I care for what you did with me now that I can't see it new again. I read you daily and covered up your claimed flaws. Hid them with scenery you found home in quickly. Say less to me. Forget this place. You took your new home there. My temple crumbled to shame. I never knew your place. But I knew you were with me all the time. Shame on me for letting you so far into it all. Couldn't save anything for myself. Every piece of the old me. Old news. Slowly removing you. Nothing in my mind is digital. That's what hurts my soul the most. You touched it at some point.

I don't remember your fingerprints but you traced my heart the days you cried.

I really just want to hear how you conquered the day
without me lifting a finger.
Not for you at least.
I let you finish your work.
By the time we came home,
Love wasn't a chore.
And you weren't staring at the rotating door.
I wasn't a cheater in a suit.
You knew I went to work in boots.
Chelsea.
They're on the pitch we watched them on TV.
Men running around a ball and a referee.
I won't plead any fifths,
Which one did you want me to open for us?
Whiskey yes.
Bring more of your successful warmth near me.
Tell me the words used to win the board. Arouse my mind.
I've spent my time my abroad in beds cleaned just for me.
We adapted to time differences long before you settled
down with me.
Distance never killed us.
It was hearing each other's voice over a speaker that did.
Forgetting nothing of your touch for I would only shake others
hands,
Couple more times till I'm next to you when I land.
New ideas after time apart.
Keeping it new with us.

The villain is the icon behind the plan.
Once he rises he'll preach a gospel that'll turn him into your hero.

The quiet live in all shades of black.
Their light remains within.
The loud bleed every color.
Absorbing all the light.

Manifest this,
Nothing leads to lifelong bliss.
For tomorrow you start new.
Yesterday's hero dies and the villain reaches out to save you.

Bring me up to put me down.
What kind of help are you?
Pick me up then put me down.
Like a bag of chips I left my taste in you.
Kiss me once and tell me was that for pleasure or to practice - For
someone other than me when they take you down on a mattress.

KISMAT

She's the blanketed warmth in the winter as you stand
shivering in defeat.
You've torn your home apart seeking her presence.
She has now graced your eyes with tears left by your
marks on skin.
You recall your anger and tremble down to your knees.
You are now where you forced her.

The only safety you find is folding hands in prayer.
Eyes closed -
The connection is only with you and the Holy one.
Asking for forgiveness or thanking Him for what he's done?
Secrecy kept between the different stories battled
through your palms.
The journey of life, you wish for it to be long reading his Psalms.
No one else to read with but others around the world like you,
read along.

I speak to the millions.
I speak to the thousands.
I speak to the hundreds.
I speak to the levels of this world.

They're all single beings.
Woven through a pattern like stars draped in skies graced
by their names.
Difference is we quantify their fame.
Whose to say their glory hasn't graced them yet?
Or if it has, how long will they remain the same as their
progression.
Each story of a building isn't drafted alike unless the top
asked for it to be so.
Badge into their mind and the cost matters.
Happiness shatters.
They have to work their way from turmoil to cleaner soil.
Each level of life...
We all can't float amongst constellations.

AARAV CHOPRA

Ring the alarm,
Sing your song.
I'll rise,
You know where our lips belong.

You wept for years,
The countless tears.
Forgotten more,
Than you ever explored.
Remembered the past,
Enough to not be able to replace your last.
Edges are corners without neighbors
Sharpen up —
You're only dull now, you'll be striking somewhere else later.

It hurts now for we weren't ready to hurt that way.
You were hurt before I arrived.
I arrived wounded to you.
We became stronger for your pain I knew how to treat.
My pain you swore I'd never repeat.

You smoked Midnight's in the morning to feel the
burn of last night.
Ashes ashes we all fall down.
Chop another one now.
Load the rest of it up with whatever will numb me back down.
Eyes low. jawline stiff.
Knuckles closed. pass off the spliff.
Higher leaf drifted speech.
To save yourself in public you call it collard greens.
Loud.
Sprinkle the crumble they say it'll turn your frown upside down.
We forgot what mattered...
Bring some more Corona's ...
Just because they were Extras and we needed brews.
Summers in the Bay.
Freestyles when the beats hit play.
So loose after the 8 hour shift we cut the noose.
Just until the high wore off again.

Studying history different than the symmetry of this world.
For they say we're balanced but we're so torn apart.
Two hands to deal the fury of minds collected in waves of
 forgotten truths.
Two feet to traverse the carnations of the fooled.
Building upon holy lands and not remembering the sacred
spaces others called peace before they preyed.
They found gold let go of the silver.
Forgot the linings we found more common.
Olive branches were akin to the nectar dancing grapes.
Spices carried throughout the world and silk torn apart to be
remade.
Traditions broken to make new.
A new world order but order was never set upon you.
Directed away from injustice they teach what the majority do.
This isn't history. There's always been a war. Materials. Beings.
Territories.
Fables don't make sense to me too.
Wanderlust teaches you more than the books do.
Experience the ripple effect to toast like they do.
Origins set apart by those who take care of you.
Sinners, villains, lovers, and caregivers alike.
Split for reasons they can't tell the clean truth.
How did we get here...

A man's belief of science and theory or the pondering souls who
say there's more to figure out but we can't for it's all unstable since
the beginning.

We burned wax for so long the only scent leftover was of our souls withering away

Remove me like the last screw knowing without me you
will not be leveled.
My mind is just as threaded into a pattern knowing how
to make it work with you.
But you no longer require me, no longer require a love so young,
you never wanted things to become old. Spoiled. Date me till I
am rotten.
Your forgotten harvest.
My last option to invest.
More of me into a seed in you.
You sent me away, I will root in you.
Severances bring peace to no one,
This time you leave me, it will not be as easy as putting the screw
back on.

We don't fall for free, we fall for freedom.
Not our kingdoms, our souls.
We stay ten toes down with those we wish to have around.

If it returns to the calling of self-worth we have found what it is to
love, but not fill us.

Why not jump? There have been barriers passed by you already.
Why not run? Did you not do so as a child? Can you carry one
as they carry you? If not altogether, one by one. Meet your match
before your maker.

You have to make room for another so they can see you in
paradise together. Accept someone. Adhere to their value next to
your name. Take them for their complete being, step by step filling
the space leftover in you.

Were you allured by the petals or how they lay atop her skin? I
hope you were curious about the reasons she let you in.

Don't stumble unless for the glass of red.
Forget the dresser, she fancies you on her bed.
Don't leave your florins for her she is gold on her own.
Just for tonight, make her feel home.

KISMAT

Riddle me love or riddle me pain.

Riddle one or the other never bother again.

Give me your hand or your last word.

Trust me I'll hold on or I'll never be heard.

After this choice you have to know,

That turning back is not an option for us to grow.

So be here presently or be my past.

I am only searching for someone who will be my last.

I want to be where your eyes rest, stuck in the glare that is the
sunlight in the room but so are you.

The layered elements around, the sheer quality of the scenery
felt similar now.

Now as I hear your voice, it's still soothing far more than the old
fashioned I had when you defended your love for me that night
here of weeks past.

*The attendant still looks at me in disgust as if I should have
let you ease up.*

*Too bad for her I love it when you just say the things that leave
me untouched.*

Away on business but focused on you, tea bags filled with love.
You picked the leaves yourselves and provided the honey too. I
am now sick and tired, not in the childish way.

I am away from my healer, to earn my honest pay.

HOME GROWN

Find me back on Liberty St.
The chandelier glow and my tiny little feet.
The fence I can't look over.
Footballs lost and never thrown back over.
The stones we mixed and matched.
The front yard we designed and couldn't have back.
It was the best.
Was but now it's just a novelty at rest.
For we lived in that home.
My childhood playground -
Home of the first band aids I've ever put on.
I miss you every now and then Emeryville.
I miss many homes, the middle class move more than
we want to...
I grew up to find out that's how it goes and it's still real.
I don't regret the changes in my life.
For I grew up on Liberty St.
I'm a free man on Earth wherever I take my feet.

Look into my eyes,
Tell what you feel inside of you.
Take this leap of faith I feel there's more left out there for us to do.
Believe me.
I saw you,
Not through you.
Applauding you.
Every little thing you do to make me better I adore you.
Challenging yourself before you tell me what you expect me to do.
I'd rather take it from a person who does than one who doesn't.
Holy Grail mind body & soul invested in you not holding back.
This isn't just about giving up myself to love.
I never gave up when you looked into my eyes and simply told me you feel this way too.
Waited my whole life for this...
This accomplishment.

SAINT VALENTINE

Bring on the clubs, bring on the stones.
I only wish to bring happiness to your homes.
I will live in secrecy for the seekers to find,
The faith I believe in can bring vision back to the blind.
Asterius knows what I am capable of,
I've shown him the way when he was to show me out.
I was not a martyr in the Colosseum to meet my cruel fate,
Claudius II and his Romans took me to the Flaminian Gate.
So I hope you read this letter signed,
"from your Valentine."
History will tell you to love me,
I was beheaded -
Long before I let all of your love shine.

Not fearing commitment,
Don't ruin my peace with your persistence.
As long as I'm in one piece.
Healthy and wise –
Single peace.

KISMAT

I feared knowledge like a fool.
I already have the tools I said running violently through
the wrong ideas.
I sharpened skills that no one should know.
Been towering over others as if I paved the best path –
Elevated alone. to be alone at last.
Show me the information I have denied.
I thought I had it right this whole time. guess it was always there.
I no longer applied.

I can't live in and out of halfway houses trying to remember what
the whole you was like?
Fearful of making you my future and leaving one eye
open at night?
Like how did this all happen and is it even true?
Did I know already as I gathered the clues.
Walking into everything I ran away from,
Rehab comes in every form.
Now I'm in a home, reborn.

KISMAT

Show me how you love.
I just might have to learn from you.
I just might take what you do and show you what
you deserve too.
Just relax this isn't the end.
We don't want to run we never had to pretend.
Room service knocking...
Leave it outside the door.
It'll take sometime to put back on our robes.
Closed corners twined hearts we came to confide.
Either way you look at the world someone's trying to hide.
Endless pride when we're side by side.
Cheers to how we love.

Before the moment the hair rises on your skin,
I've seen your soul chill for mine and welcome me in.
Feathery touch -
Just enough to make you do more than blush.
This isn't a matter not involving trust,
For tonight we feed on our lust.

If it was all about the money most wouldn't want to see you later.
Paper chaser.
If you let down your walls and made deposits for your heart,
that's a start.
We've been up and down and jaded over payments can you see,
life is more about you than the money trees.
You can make it all life long but not love.
People love you when you flaunt it just know that doesn't carry
above.
Not from the heart, unless it's a gift.
Don't worry about it all monetarily, love isn't something
that can split.
Unless it's 50-50 with them,
No credit check, no scams.
If you love them then make memories priceless and take them to
heaven.

Do you know about the shadows in the distance...they're headed for you.

Stormy eyes, ruined the surprise, lightning scripting out the torment of your soul split in two.

One side this, the other that, no other way to define it.

Sometimes, you live and you learn to fill the other bits.

Either way, the shadows are headed your way, it's best to prepare now so you can get over it.

KISMAT

I forgot my roots.
Through broken truths.
Either way I see it.
The way I live you lose.
Why me?
Why not you? --
Is something I never ask.
I want you to gain credit for the completed task -
Heartbeats chasing the breathes. whose to say who gets their last?
Raise the masts...
Let's sail.
I'm no captain.
Direction was never my gift babe.
Life boats are man made -
I ask you to dive.....
Why you ask....
I've sailed and sailed...
Your soul was mine to save.

Popping excessively to escape the chilling demons who don't fit in
their capsules anymore.
Cannot shake them off your skin, leaving a trail in your
bloodstream where they seek your score.
Adding up doses like points, trade them back and forth your
sobriety is fleeting with each choice.
Different colors in the bag pick one up to rejoice.
Altered states, irregular breaths.
Heaviness is what you want to feel in the end.
Or would you rather float vividly so you can pretend they weren't
real in your head.
Heavens message is to live with the proper balance,
Name off the prescriptions -
Take it down with whatever's left in the chalice.
Acting like an addict who cannot manage two steps without
another added -
Dose.
I can breathe in hope, as I exhale the dope.
I can now cope.

KISMAT

There's no way to fall into it the right way.
Slipped right out of your hands again -
I'd crave for more attention.
But I am your bittersweet
Like marmalade you'll jar me for weeks.
Maybe I thought I'd win but I can't swim.
How will I ever float?
When I don't breathe. I choke.
Don't you?
Do I scorn myself or let you keep doing what you do?

You are your actuality.
Sometimes you are off kilter but that is not an
abnormality.
Read and react they taught you that, what you give does not
always come back.
So much for that.
Believe in the action like you do yourself.
If you don't now, the day will come to love yourself.
Inhibitions tend to create habits that reveal the opposite
side of you.
Don't let your past dictate your future and never think of your
future expectations as if you've solved it all as something that will
come true.
Never change.
Never change.
Never change.
If not for yourself to grow wiser with the accepted past that
comes with your age.

Anything that you do is to live for your well being. There is no reason to doubt the person you become. Never should you think that you are a lesser person from the experiences that made you who you are today. You're no runaway. You made a way.

Whichever way you were able to handle it, you did. You were dealt the cards you were given, and you became this way to handle each scenario with what you learned to be the best response.

With or without the help of your family.
They may call you names and label you but stand by your experiences and they may teach you more than what they've carried you through already.

Life allowed you opportunities and experiences to grow and expand your being and exercise very specific and custom muscles just for you. No one can do what you do the way you do.

You made choices, they yielded strengths and results, it was all you, always all you. Life led you a certain way just for you, take those affluences and learnings and run freely in your power, run with it.

The focus is not the circumstance, not the people or what they did, or what 'happened to you.' It all happened for you, the focus is on you and your choices. The focus is on you, always you.

Every evening they ask about you?
Where you are, how you do, how you feel about being you?
May that be too persistent -
We cannot say we're perfect.
Forgive the remarks, we've all made many.
But you can cross each one off if you found their lips.
Space does teach you this.
Not much is said unless it's sealed with a true kiss.
Until next time, it's still you -
I miss.

The most magical part about you is indeed the silver lining to
learning about the shine leftover in you.
Sometimes you wrap yourself up in a blanket.
The warmth only helps cover your eyes from the day.
If you rise out of the blankets and look at the warmth of the sun
like your will to life.
Each step will help you shine -
The room will only stay bright until you come home tonight.

I used to tread lightly, confident yet holding on to some of the
grievances held inside of me.
Stripping apart the papers mentally locked so deep in me.
I swear to you all I've ever asked for was a family.
I have now found mine and the steps are now taken with them in
mind you see.
I see those locked away abnormalities, turned into modern day
clean realities.
My depression has been swept clean by their hearts filling the
holes in me.
I found myself in family.
No longer will I lock myself in my mind and worry.

Where would the world go if the angels never tried to feed the
devils though?
Truest form of love creating no barrier with the misaligned.
Some may believe in arrows to harm, some may believe in the
bows string to break before they harm too many.
No matter how much you can give or take, sometimes a wound-
ed soul only needs a single plate.
I've heard stories I can retell but never relate.
But anytime a meal was involved, people rejoiced that day.

He learned to carry on his name.
Devils cast him down for shame.
The man they could always blame.
Someone they willingly sent pain.
Yet he did what he always did and overcame.
The devil's lost their battle and could no longer tame.
The hero kept his name.
The story never changed,
He kept the turmoil in to prove he's still the same.
Humble and undefeated.

Had to look beyond your eyes,
To see the creation of God.
A body full wisdom and the healing touch in your arms.
Fingers laced with prints I want over me.
Embrace me softly then hold onto my pain.
I'll let go of what I've held for something new with your name.
Something new with your name.

AARAV CHOPRA

I let you linger in my mind
Sit between my nerves
Show me something new -
whenever you wanted to.
I sat because I couldn't move
Meditating through the peace in you.

The subtle insecurities I was raised with are still there.
How I must not speak when the man in the room is yelling.
How his tone can aggress more than just me and I must listen.
How I should run to the highest places to feel safe.
I have grown to now emulate the male pain.
The yelling and bond severing.
I couldn't be the shield.
I wanted to fight.
So I became the anger.
I never learned how to defuse anything.

I wish to speak to the angels layered in the feathers
graced by God.
I want to know why they were chosen and how
their bodies changed to carry souls.
Do they float amongst the clouds away from the ones they love?
Was it a passage or a right?
Do they sing in union or have to battle for their kingdom when
danger is in sight?
Do repenting demons line up for their wings?
At the gates of hell who really holds their sadness while
burning
-
Will they not remain raging?
I'm torn between the scriptures for on Earth we send demons
away for life.
If we're all God's children...
How does one get wings while the other burns?
Is there any even count in the afterlife?
We'll never know.

KISMAT

You came undone -
I have you released.
Conquered your sadness with my own shade of madness.
You chose it.
So you won't be with him...
Not to win.
Not to sin.
Not to grin.
Not to remain thin hearted within.
I know it's there.
Just divine intervention taking care of your time.
Having you here, calling you mine.
Unraveling the truth between your thighs
Whispering to make him your past.

You've finally been touched the way you want at last

Told my mother I'll go see the world one day,
With her kindred spirit following me to honor my ways.
I can't deceive any souls.
There's a definite story left to be told.
I wish to tell her all the way she'd wish,
Her eyes will always glisten.
I'll remember her everywhere -
She won't be lost in my bliss.

No sleep so I caved into the almost empty tank of adrenaline. Still
wake up before my alarm no doubt show up to work make sure
the coffee pot is full thanks to the person who made it. Sometimes
I'm too tired to even change the filter, I'm living off kilter.
Maybe the negatives in my sleep bank accounts,
Everybody wants my sale for free,
Yet they have money they can make and count.
They don't understand the predicaments of a hard working man.
Whose only right is your transaction through the phone, card
security code.

Yeah...
That's me,
Everyday,
Closing the everyday man.

Stress me out wear me thin.
I'll keep on. you'll never win.
Easy going –
I never was.
I'll sign my name to the work.
Below and above.

KISMAT

They never wanted to save you
Forget the thought of getting what you deserved.
Swerve around the wrong lanes and ask yourself how'd
you get home –
Worried about your safety instead of what happened.
Laying in bed sound asleep until you try to remember
what's been lost in your head.
You forgot your own values and let the bottle tell you your truths.
The bottle is empty but the label can't provide the level of proof
to your clues.
Forgot how to tie your own noose forget about it.
This life you can't lose.
If it requires a bottle bottom out your pride.
You never needed liquor -
You just asked to feel alive.

The beauty that you show...Protects me from the pain.

Your heart...met my soul...I lost all my words.

The seasons come and go...

You fell from the sky...

I see you in the light...you saved me from the burns.

The cruel world has left a burden and the beauty of
your soul...protects.

They look but they should know...my eyes are lost in yours.

They see me and they know....that I....am yours.

If I couldn't take it anymore you'll be there with open arms.

I'll never forget the person that you are in my life.

I use to runaway from the tears but now you have shaken the fear.
It disappeared.

They see me and they know....that I....am yours.

KISMAT

Tell me why you're here...
Why you chose to come back?
I've went ahead and bettered myself - fixed all the
things you said I lacked. I believed you at some point in time.
Your word meant more to me than anyone else in mind.
I thought I was doing it to please you but truthfully it was never
enough. I smiled more. cared more. still did all the things you
loved and watched you fall asleep. I put your demons to rest
every night so you didn't wake up weak. I let you do as wish
because it all made sense to me when you kissed my lips.
The pain has left from the images of you.
The sadness I kept faded away like the scent of you.
So I ask again, why are you here?
Simply because you were in the area and shed a couple tears?
I'm no longer yours - I'm here because I chose to protect.
The place that I call home. the sanctuary that you left.

Nothing but liquor courage in a cabinet heart.
Locked away with pure emotions.
She passes through me and I fade away.
Losing control of what I should say... feeling some type of way.
She's the aura I haven't found.
Something I can't pick up off the ground.
Elevation never feared me but getting high off a being did.
Something more complex.
We can't satisfy each other with just sex.
We'll pass over to the next day with a memory laying next
to each other in bed.
But did I earn a spot in your head?
I softly ran my fingers across your chest, whispering sweet noth-
ings and tracing your heart over your breast.
Never felt so safe giving you all I am. Tongue tied no longer.
But where will I end up next summer...will this be the end
of loves game.
Will I be burning up with you or somewhere drinking away your
name?

KISMAT

I watch people cook white lies right in front of me.
I'm not surprised that's my reality.
For I've done my share of dishonesty.
Beat the drum
Pour me some drinks
Honesty hour has kicked in.
Truth between your eyes I can't see it
So I listen in
Just until you're okay again.
Allow me to drift into the bourbon.
Okay.
Now let's figure out where you went wrong I grabbed
some paper and my Parker pen.
You're now baking lies.
Serving them after you've frozen them in you.
What's the cost of me standing nearby you?
Toxicity.
Longevity.
Envy.
More pain.
Sorrowful madness.
I'm blending tears with the ink from my pen.
My assessment, I'm over it.
We're the same.
We have gone this far,
To blame each other again.
Honest people individually.
Together a liars symphony.

If you choose to be reborn.
Would you choose the same form?

INTO THE WOODS

The woods no longer provided substance to you so you came to
the suburbs.

You saw all the glam away from nature and appreciated
its false hope.

Because Sally Mae still hasn't gotten her call from that jock
we warned her about.

The jock himself is perusing through adult magazines right now...
I'm not kidding –

There goes another six dollars from his debit account.

He's a prime time collector.

The kids still hate the way school food smells too.

They still get bullied left and right as if it's a part of the curriculum.

The suburbs are not for you my dear.

Let me explain as I am now a member of the woods.

Long story still scripting I will show you the meaning of
nature in you.

I'll show you the roots in you that you didn't know existed.

I'll live it for the first time and you can vicariously share my highs.
albeit an experience you've grown into.

The story doesn't need to change all the time.

You can visit Sally Mae or I can take you to the same spot I catch
the jock nearby.

Or we can peak the mountains every Sunday and catch the
sunsets every night.

You can toss me into the river bend and I'll still chase after you.

That cabin in the woods. that's ours.

Protected from the upbeat neighborhoods. for we tell no lies.

If I could cast arrows at you I would.
But I'll write these words, they serve the same purpose.
Now tell me where I struck you first?

THE DIARY OF AN OLD FLAME

We never held hands in public the way we meant in private as her
nails left marks on my back at times. The strict passion of nightfall
withered away by daylight.

Every morning a hoodie went missing as I would hear her engine
turn over the through the blinds where I could see her cupping
her hands in front of her for warmth. At that moment we were
both cold.

I would rise to see that she did leave the way she came but a bit
more disturbed every time. I was losing a woman I loved to a
tragedy I was unable to make sense of at the time.

She would return some nights brighter a bit more relaxed but I
could sense that I was not her source for immediate relief any-
more. I wasn't her daylight. I was her night. The sun showed her
true colors. I would always miss them all. They faded away with
each kiss before sunrise.

—

I took the back roads today but not the same ones. This one felt
familiar except I was a bit more lost now than I was when I would
go to you.

There were new curves and bends. A couple new signs that said
danger lied ahead.

The gears shifted themselves this time. If you were still

around you knew I had moved closer to you manually.

I had all the power at my hands and I swear to you if the speed I traveled to love you showed you how fast I wished I could run on my own two feet you'd never let me run out of your fuel. But now my automatic setting removed me from any joy in loving a new way. Guess I was a lost disaster thinking the area code I was driving in raised me but I left my heart in yours.

My eyes fooled me as I came home to another empty bed. Guess I did take the back roads again tonight. I miss your curves. I miss our bends. We were under construction too long. The whole journey was to come to an end.

—

Remember the day we drove to the town with the reservations made and you were surprised to find out. That I had planned a night so splendid you probably took more shots in life by now to forget it. The girls were there. The guys were there too. If you know the night in memory as much as I do I'd have cut ties with one since we parted off I hope you already knew. And if you do, ask him what the best part of it all is and divide and conquer my words against his. I felt each pin drop that night. The bowling alley was next you know? One by one we knocked them down. In the end, I'm the ghost with the frown.

This may not end. There is no debauchery greater than the loss of time.

MY INABILITY

There was only a shadow of doubt and grit between her eyes that night. She either walked away profusely denying what I say as she knocked more of my things around as I lay still or her telling me how her life was great outside of my scruffy neck; away from her senses of my present indecency. Immediately I knew you were neglecting who I was when I met you. You went after my inability to change to who you said to be. I never left your side how else would you judge change.

My neck size remained the same for years but I could sense you wanted to tighten things up. It was a new age taste you wanted me to spice up to but I still looked at denim and rolled sleeves like my go to. I'm no suit and tie connoisseur and we lost touch in sweatshirts and hoodies where you would just lay on my lap exchange quick doses of love till we'd fall asleep and enjoy the nightcap. What happened to those days? Then I struggled less to love you now you've lost yourself in the glamour of life and forgot the dirt that made you one with me. I use to dress drown to leave eyes on you. Comfortably speaking you held their eyes longer and I was happy to be your man. What you don't get is...I wouldn't have it any other way. You've always been my spotlight. I'll follow you as you shine I never seek to take what lights my way. But I'll keep the scruff, roll up my sleeves, walk around in my denim to make this a reality I can believe.

I don't want you to bleed.
I've already left the ink on these pages to heal you.

Shukriya!

थँक योउ

THANK YOU

This is it, you've made it.

I am proud of you for picking up a brand new authors first book and devouring it whole. For treating this like something worth finishing. For making me feel like my efforts are valued and my heart should be heard. I hope you took something away from my catharsis. I never imagined I would be here. Honestly, who is checking on your own dreams if not yourself.

I would not be here if it wasn't for the many individuals who never let me stop. Who told me that it wasn't the end of the road when I was ready to give up before the hills needed to be passed. Who didn't stop me when the hills led to mountains and those mountains led to cliffs. They told me to fly. So I did.

This is my one story. It may have stretched far beyond fate itself but these words are what make my life pure. These pieces complete me. I let go of so much and as long as I resonate with your soul in some way or another I have satisfied my need as a writer.

I don't need you to throw me up in lights. I'd rather sit in your thoughts and be someone you can rely on for words that spark imagery, love, and deeper connection to self.

Forever grateful for someone like you.

It has been a pleasure creating Kismat, take care and I look forward to doing this again in a new light.

CPSIA information can be obtained
at www.ICGtesting.com
Printed in the USA
LVOW10s1123260218
567729LV00016B/3/P